PERSPECTIVES

PERSPECTIVES

Sex

Brenda Hadley

Rev. date: 07/16/2016

To order additional copies of this book, contact:
Xlibris
1-888-795-4274
www.Xlibris.com
Orders@Xlibris.com
745840

This is dedicated to my boyz Tyrece,Tyson, Andre Jr. my queen Lasharra, my Pastor Eugene Overstreet ,family friends of Golden Gate and my two princesses you know who you are C and N love ya Jesus loves you more.

CONTENTS

There is a common thing, something we share that's happening all over the world. Everything around us is about sex, money paid for sex, power sex, movies sex, music sex, adult entertainment magazines promoting sex, the clothes we wear say let's go have sex. We are living in a world of Sexually Transmitted (contagious) diseases such as Chlamydia, Gonorrhea, Crabs and (pubic lice), also those that have no cure like HIV, AIDS and Herpes to name a few.

Children are born, their parents don't bother to get married, the mother's give them their daddy's last name and play husband and wife and live together without shame.

The differences between male and female are confusing, when we are looking at what we think is a woman, is a man, when we are looking at a man it's a woman. Our men are seeking to be in a relationship with other men just as the woman seeks the love and attention of another woman.

Look in your Bible at <u>ROMANS 1:26,27,28</u> It says from the <u>New International</u> version or <u>Contemporary English</u> version which are written in words you can understand without the thee, thy and thou shalt not words of the <u>King James</u> version which

I only suggest once you start reading and studying you will be able to understand, which I must say is my favorite version. Okay now let's see what the Bible says <u>ROMANS 1:26,27,28</u> (26) GOD LET THEM(us)FOLLOW THEIR OWN EVIL DESIRES, WOMEN NO LONGER WANTED TO HAVE SEX IN A NATURAL WAY AND THEY DID THINGS WITH EACH OTHER THAT WERE NOT NATURAL.(27) MEN BEHAVED IN THE SAME WAY, THEY STOPPED WANTING TO HAVE SEX WITH WOMEN AND HAD STRONG DESIRES FOR SEX WITH OTHER MEN, THEY DID SHAMEFUL THINGS WITH EACH OTHER AND WHAT HAS HAPPENED TO THEM IS PUNISHMENT FOR THEIR FOOLISH DEEDS.(28) SINCE

THESE PEOPLE REFUSED EVEN TO THINK ABOUT GOD, HE ^(GOD) LET THEIR ^(OUR) USELESS MINDS RULE OVER THEM ^(US) THAT'S WHY THEY ^(WE) DO ALL SORTS OF INDECENT (FILTHY, DIRTY, NASTY) THINGS.

Before we go on we need to go way back to the beginning, some of us just don't like History, I was one who didn't care about it in school, my attitude was who cares what happened to people way before my time, I didn't know-em, its not hard to guess what kind of grade I got, How could I pass? When the teacher was trying to teach me I came from Homo-Sapiens (ape to man) they lost me right there. I remember we were shown a diagram of an ape like man walking bent over, as the pictures went on the ape face faded into a man standing straight and no longer bent over, I think they really believed all that craziness. I remember going to Sunday School taught me how I was created, Thank God for the Pastor and teachers I probably would of believed I came from and ape. (lol) Now let's get some real true history in us or a refreshing of the mind for some.

How Man Can To Be

We need to remember that God created the first man on the sixth day the world was created. (To learn how the world was created read the first book in the Bible

Genesis 1:1-31) Lets read where Adam the first man was created go to GENESIS 2:6,7(6) BUT STREAMS CAME UP FROM THE EARTH AND WATERED THE WHOLE SURFACE OF THE GROUND. (7) AND THE LORD GOD FORMED MAN OF THE DUST OF THE GROUND AND BLEW INTO HIS NOSTRILS THE BREATH OF LIFE AND MAN BECAME A LIVING SOUL (Adam) The mist gave moisture to the dirt, the kind of moisture the dirt had for building sand castles on the beach with a child, it can be pressed an formed to what shapes you want. God took the dirt formed man into an image of himself, that's power for sure, then blew his breath into the nostrils of man made from dirt, from Gods hand he came alive. (Adam)

If people living in this day saw such a thing being done by God a lot of us would think God did some type of new illusion or magic trick like magicians Houdini and Chris Angel, But only through the Mighty Power of God we as human beings are blessed the day Air of Life was blown gently into the nose of a man made of dirt. Breathe In, Breathe Out that's the life God gave us, we can be thankful for that alone, each day is another breath of life.

How Woman Came To Be

GENESIS 2:18 THEN THE LORD SAID IT'S NOT GOOD FOR THE MAN TO BE ALONE. I WILL MAKE HIM A HELPER SUITABLE FOR HIM. Now go to GENESIS 2:21,22,23,25 (21 SO THE LORD GOD CAUSED THE MAN (Adam) TO FALL INTO A DEEP SLEEP, AND WHILE HE WAS SLEEPING, (Adam) HE (God) TOOK ONE OF THE MANS (Adams) RIBS AND CLOSED UP THE PLACE WITH FLESH. (22) THEN THE LORD GOD MADE A WOMAN FROM THE RIB HE HAD TAKEN OUT OF THE MAN AND HE (God) BROUGHT HER TO THE MAN. (Adam) (23) THE MAN (Adam) SAID THIS IS BONE OF MY BONES FLESH OF MY FLESH, SHE

SHALL BE CALLED WOMAN FOR SHE WAS TAKEN OUT OF MAN.

Isn't that something the first man created was also the first man to have surgery the doctor (God) used His anesthesia (Power) to put Adam in a deep sleep opened up his side took out a rib bone and closed him back up. God is so amazing if he hadn't taken a rib out of Adams own body I as a woman would never existed. We a women should always remember that Gods All Mighty Power made man from the mist of water and dirt then went inside he man's flesh removed one rib bone to create me (you) a woman, the one and only time a woman would come from a man, I thank God for the life of a woman's existence men you should also remember God said it is <u>Not Good</u> for man to be alone and also the woman was made to be a help mate not someone to give orders to or call your property but to be a help to you.

<u>GENESIS 2:25</u> THE MAN AND HIS WIFE WERE BOTH NAKED AND THEY FELT KNOW SHAME

To be fruitful (To produce a lot of- to make) and multiply (To increase in number, To breed mate animals) or reproduce (Have children) Read <u>GENESIS 1:28</u> AND GOD BLESSED THEM SAYING BE FRUITFUL AND MULTIPLY, It wasn't until after Adam and Eve disobeyed God that sex was messed up by the shame of what they did.(Ate from the Tree of Knowledge of Good and Evil).

The World Sentenced To Die

To be seen without any clothes on will make us feel shame, if it isn't our husband or wife, boyfriend or girlfriend we want to hide ourselves, we don't want anybody looking at us. To find out why we get so embarrassed when we are seen naked read <u>GENESIS 3:1-24</u>, That would be all of chapter 3.

The first verse in chapter 6 of Genesis tells us more and more people were born and were spread all over the earth (World). Now let's go to <u>GENESIS 6:5,6,7</u> (5)THE LORD GOD SAW HOW BAD THE PEOPLE ON EARTH WERE, AND EVERYTHING THEY THOUGHT AND PLANNED WAS EVIL.(6)HE (God) WAS VERY SORRY THAT HE MADE THEM (people) AND HE (God) SAID I'LL (I will) DESTROY EVERY LIVING CREATURE ON EARTH I'LL (I will) WIPE OUT (Get rid of) PEOPLE, ANIMALS, BIRDS AND REPTILES I'M SORRY I EVER MADE THEM.

Think back to a time when you did something wrong and the person you never wanted to know how you been really acting all out here in the world suddenly found out. I'm gonna share something I had done. I was 18 years old, you couldn't tell me anything, I had an answer for everything, if you asked me I really thought I had my self together. I was in the world doing me. I was doing what I wanted to do. I was a lil hustler baby that's what I am a hustler baby I want you to know that's who I am, oh yeah! I was a hot mess back then, I was always thinking of ways to get money, not make money, get money without laying on my back, a hooker, ho, prostitute whatever you want to call it, I had to much jazzy class to be one not to say I was ever called one before or even picked up a charge, Instead of getting caught with selling dope a ho charge was the one you would rather have to keep from doing a lot of time in jail. My brain was thinking if you can make a mistake when you type on paper (Yeah we used a typewriter back in the not too far day) anyway you make a mistake an used a white correction liquid to cover the mistake, needless to say I'm not here to teach you how to be a bad person, I made money orders appear more than what they were an cashed them in,(sad to say I looked innocent but was very corrupt) when my father found out I was taken to jail by him, I remember the look of hurt and disappointment on his face as he gave me over to the police, the pain in his eyes, I can only imagine how he felt, was he ashamed he ever took part in me being born? Suppose he wished I was never born.

If you thought of something evil you have done, well we know if it was something wrong it was evil and if its evil its bad, and your father found out suppose he can just get rid of you because you are too wicked to be around others.

Look and see all around us the attitudes we have are in a hurry to do nothing. We only got time for our plans. We stay on the subject on how we gonna get money to get an even better car, bigger house and even more money just to keep up with each other instead of how to use money properly. Some people are losing their lives because they either don't have money to give or they just got too much of it. If we bump into each other of stand in one another's way, instead of a simple excuse me I'm sorry we won't even say that's alright and have a good day.

As you will notice how we are living in a world now full of wickedness that the Lord saw in GENESIS 6:5-7 The Lord was so hurt and upset look at verse 7 and HE SAID, I'LL (I will) DESTROY EVERY LIVING CREATURE ON EARTH I'LL (I will) WIPE OUT PEOPLE BIRDS AND REPTILES I'M SORRY I EVER MADE THEM

At this time in life there were no laws set in place if you did something wrong. Can you imagine how the world would be if we had no laws to live by? You stole something or just walked up to someone that had something you wanted and you took it from them and nothing would or could be done about it, you see people fighting and killing each other, so what who gonna stop us? Sounds like a very noisy mean cruel world. It's like some of the streets across many states right now to this very day we won't be caught on for fear of what could happen to us if we turn on the wrong block in a dangerous neighborhood which don't even compare to how the people acted in GENESIS 6:5,6. The one who created everything (God) has that same power to destroy everything.

If we don't like our old run down car we <u>get rid of it,</u> we get tired of the clothes we bought last week <u>we get rid of them</u>, we can get rid of just about anything we want, we cook something we don't like or we burn we throw it out <u>get rid of it.</u>

God created everything, he made us, he didn't like how wicked people had become so what did he do? He got rid of them! <u>GENESIS 6:8-22</u>, <u>GENESIS 7:1-24</u> and <u>GENESIS 9:1-29</u>, The one who obeyed God was Noah these scriptures above are the story of how the first world population was destroyed by a flood down to one family, I encourage you to go back and read. Go to <u>GENESIS 7:21,22</u>

(21) NOT A BIRD, ANIMAL, REPTILE OR HUMAN WAS LEFT ALIVE ANYWHERE ON EARTH. (22) THE LORD DESTROYED EVERYTHING THAT BREATHED.

The World Starting All Over Again

The Lord started the world again with Noah and his family, this time saying in GENESIS 9:7 AS FOR YOU BE FRUITFUL AND INCREASE IN NUMBER, MULTIPLY ON THE EARTH AND INCREASE UPON IT.

GENESIS 10:1 AFTER THE FLOOD (Noah's sons) SHEM, HAM AND JEPHETH HAD MANY DESCENDANTS, they obeyed God to be fruitful and multiply, Noah's sons produced families, cities, states and entire nations to repopulate the earth all over the world. Think about the nations today, we should keep in mind we are all Red, Yellow, Black and White part of the same family (Adam and Eve) descended from the same righteous man (Noah) <u>GENESIS 10:32</u>.

<u>Beginning Of Laws</u>

Exodus 2 to Deuteronomy 34 Is the beginning of the story up until his death of another great man that would be all the books of Exodus, Leviticus, Numbers and Deuteronomy, these books are about a man named Moses who through Gods instructions led Israel to freedom from slavery in

Egypt and gave the nation God's law. I encourage you to read about him.

The beginning of laws that we are to live by to this very day were based on the Ten Commandments Exodus 20:1-17, Deuteronomy 5:1-21 from God himself. The people were so afraid they wanted Moses to speak to them instead of God, Moses receives the Laws of God and presents it to the people (something to go back and read).

The three commandments I will be referring to are: Honoring or Respecting your parents: Exodus 20:12/Deuteronomy 5:16 with scriptures including instructions to the parents. Do Not Commit

Adultery (Which is don't be unfaithful in marriage) Exodus 20:4/Deuteronomy 5:18 with scriptures on fornication and other topics relating to our sexual conduct. Do Not Covet (which is don't want what belongs to another).

Children's Respect

E X O D U S - 2 0 : 1 2 , DEUTERONOMY-5:16 HONOR YOUR FATHER AND MOTHER (parents) THAT YOUR DAYS MAY BE PROLONGED. (that you may live long in the land which the Lord God gave you).

EHESIANS 6:1,2,3 [1] CHILDREN YOU BELONG TO THE LORD AND YOU DO THE RIGHT THING WHEN YOU OBEY YOUR PARENTS.[2] HONOR YOUR FATHER AND MOTHER- WHICH IS THE FIRST COMMANDMENT WITH A PROMISE.[3]AND YOU WILL HAVE A LONG AND HAPPY LIFE.

Some of us came from homes that left painful memories of our childhood. We may find it hard to think kind words towards our parents, we may not like what our mothers or fathers have done or haven't done to us or with us.

Some never cared or just didn't have time to bother with us, but we all have some type of memory of when our parents tried to teach us right from wrong even if they weren't there some of us had our grandparents, Respect your parents even though they (we) have faults. Disrespecting our parents can have terrible consequences for our lives. To live long is to have respect for how your (our) life came from two people your mother and your father. R-E-S-P-E-C-T we all know what it means to be.

PROVERBS 13:1 CHILDREN WITH GOOD SENSE ACCEPT CORRECTION FROM THEIR PARENTS, BUT

STUBBORN CHILDREN IGNORE IT COMPLETELY.

Stop Your Clock(Time) For Your Children

PROVERBS 22:6 TRAIN UP A CHILD IN THE WAY HE SHOULD GO AND WHEN HE IS OLD HE WILL NOT TURN FROM IT.

EPHESIANS 6:4 PARENTS DON'T BE HARD ON YOUR CHILDREN RAISE THEM PROPERLY, TEACH THEM AND INSTRUCT THEM ABOUT THE LORD.

When we were children we were taught not to lie, steal and cheat and also to be kind to people by our parents, grandparents, aunts, uncles, brother, sisters, god parents, foster parents, coaches, teachers and pastors of our churches. For the "you didn't say who taught me" isn't on the list people, maybe its because you thought you raised yourself.

Parents today entertain their children with Playstations, X-Boxes, I-pods, I-Pads and any other electronic gadgets also to include the electronic babysitter the Big Screen TV and its accessories, DVD Player with boxes of movies most of them boot-leg ouch! Gotta keep it real, Y'all know most of us were not going to the store, we checked in with our movie man to see if he got the movie we wanted, if he didn't have it he could burn ya one (make a copy) while we waited. Yeah we all were and are doing a little piracy huh? (lol) We didn't have time to fly a kite with our children, didn't have time to ride a bike with our children, didn't have time to go see our children in the school play or hear them say their speeches at Christmas and Easter programs at church. We didn't have time to just stop and listen to our children on anything, We didn't even have time to teach our children, instead we put a band-aid or temporary fix on our guilt by buying things because our grown-up problems we were having seem to come first and to some we just got too busy to check in on our children.

I Tried

To the parents who many were the only one there to provide for their child or children, a lot of us tried our very best with raising them to live by the Bibles moral standards, like I mentioned earlier, Don't take what don't belong to you, don't lie to your parents or other people, don't copy answers from somebodies paper to pass a test cause that's cheating, don't play a game you make sure you win all the time cause that's selfish and a wrong attitude to have, and don't get mad because your friend got a new car and you still walking, now you hope they have an accident and can't drive, the list goes on and on. We tried to teach our children instead of them listening they chose to go from not paying attention to doing what they wanted to do, Why did this happen? They did exactly what we did, grew up and got to grown to listen to our parents telling us how to live our life so they(we) went out to find their(our) own way of life only to be found by people doing all sorts of drugs and drinking designer drinks to get them(us) drunk and high just to fit in with the I'm down for the anything crowd, more and more babies are born to this group of people of various ages, ethnic backgrounds and economic status which means this is going on to the rich and poor alike.

Sex Education

If I was taught clearer, if the teachers explained the outcome of what will happen instead of what <u>could</u> happen, or how a man and woman's body parts work together to make a baby in Health Class just maybe I would of made better choices. All I remember was my teaching pointing at fallopian tubes and the uterus and the scrotum and penis of the man drawn without skin to make us feel like we were looking at the inside of our bodies, all I noticed was veins and muscles, no skin, no bones.(lol) I guess the teachers did the best they could. The doctors even tried to help when someone invented a pill to prevent females from having children which only taught us its ok to have sex but <u>practice</u> safe sex, learn how to practice safe sex, be safe, then you can have all the sex you want without making a baby yea!!! But to the girls, if you did slip up and get pregnant, Do you think the person you laid down with will claim he's the father and take responsibility for a child he help bring into this world? If he's the father that pokes his chest all out playing daddy only when others are around, Can you count the diapers, formula and sleepless nights only invested by you the mother, was it really worth it?

We know our children learn about sex, the problem is who or what is teaching them at home, school and church and at what age are they being taught? The exposure of sexual situations the children see on television shows, movies and even the cartoons are teaching its ok to have sexy things on the mind. We as parents should always be concerned we should take the time and just do our part, after all everything a child begins to know starts at the home.

Parental Control

We all know about parental control through the experiences we had growing up. Were we allowed to watch anything we wanted on TV? No! we could not, as a matter of fact we had a time frame when we were allowed to do everything we did, Y'all remember before cable networks started popping up all over the country we had 4 to 5 channels to look at, back then we didn't have what programs that were coming on scrolling down the television screen, we had the famous TV Guide with programs scheduled to be aired for the day and the rest of the week, there were know televisions in every room of our houses. I remember we would come if from school put on play clothes, get a snack which would probably of been a Peanut Butter & Jelly sandwich, Peanut Butter or Bologna and Cheese with crackers or an apple, orange or banana, that was a snack not a Pizza, Doughnuts, Cake & Ice Cream which when we had that it was somebodies Birthday. After the snack came the house chores, when you got all that done and had your homework from school done you could look at a cartoon show, Zoom, Mr. Rogers in the Neighborhood, Electric Company & Sesame Street which were for the most learning programs that lasted 30 minutes. Most of our time was spent playing outside, everybody knew how to tell playground time by the color the sky changed you better be home before the street light came on! (lol) We got our clothes ready for school, took a bath and watched whatever your mama had on the channel for you to look at and you didn't give up any lip cause that would get your head almost knocked off and a faster trip to go to bed, if it was left up to our daddy's we would be in bed as soon as we took our baths they didn't care about us looking at know TV, I believe they thought it was meant for them to watch football, basketball, baseball and a good match-up of two men boxing, wrestling and boring golf.

When the television was put into every bedroom our parents gave up their control to allow us to make our own choices to what programs or TV shows we wanted to watch, this was the start of all TV networks competing with each other offering more and even better programs until the TV Guide no longer exist. Now we have the internet to type the word SEX and thousands to millions now billions of information can be easily downloaded at our fingertips from the privacy of our home mainly the bedroom and we wonder why our children are hanging out in their bedrooms behind closed doors instead of playing outside, Sex education this way is damaging our children's minds. Let's remember a child's first education about sex should start at home with the parents. As little children we were taught the parts of our body an how to use them. The main thing our mother's drilled in our little brains was for us girls our coo coo, tee tee, pocketbooks whatever names were used was private, you don't talk about your body parts in a bad way and most of all <u>nobody</u> should <u>touch</u> our private parts and we better not <u>show</u> our body parts. To the boys they were told the same but also not to be mannish.

Before puberty (signs your body's changing) a girl needs to know her body is going to change into a young lady why and how menstruation happens. A boy needs to know that his body is changing into a young man and he should know about nocturnal emission (wet dreams) happens sometimes. A boy and girl at this age should be told that nothing is wrong with them and that it's the natural developments happening to their bodies with boys and girls their ages. When a child starts to notice their bodies changing they should already have been taught the values of reading and living by what the Bible says and how important it is to do so. What the Bible teaches about sex is worth learning, once you have read it then you too will know and be able to help those who are confused about what the Bible says about sex. Instead of listening to what others have to say I suggest that you read the Bible for yourself, look up the scriptures through-out these pages, find out what it really teaches about sex.

Go to <u>SONGS OF SOLOMON 2:7,3:5, 8:4</u> (3 times this verse is mentioned) DAUGHTERS OF JERUSALEM I CHARGE YOU BY THE GAZELLES AND BY THE DOES (baby deer) OF THE FIELD DO NOT ABUSE OR AWAKEN LOVE UNTIL IT SO DESIRES.

Teaching to have protected sex has left our schools while being a virgin is laughed at. The tingly googly feelings young people have are mistaken for love, these are the same feelings we had as youth when we started to like someone and we got chill bumps or gushy feelings then we thought it was

Love til they broke up with ya, now ya hurt can't eat or sleep for thinking about the one you gave your heart to. We just weren't taught about not letting ourselves get aroused or even think about sex until the right time, we did what we saw instead of waiting, we had a hit it and run attitude.

ROMANS 6:12 DON'T LET SIN RULE YOUR BODY, YOUR BODYS BOUND TO DIE SO DON'T OBEY ITS DESIRES

With God's help our young adult children can hold on to one of their most precious gifts (sex) until the right time with the right person in the right relationship. They need to know how to act and how sex fits into a young person's life. If you think they are having sex now it's important to talk about the choices we make. Sex is special and exciting if you wait til you are <u>MARRIED.</u>

Teens have a lot of peer pressure the first thing they think is everybody's doing it. <u>1 CORINTHIANS 15:33</u> DON'T FOOL YOURSELVES, BAD FRIENDS WILL DESTROY YOU. We know when something we are doing is wrong but we want to please the crowd we are hanging with, we want to be popular or the happening one. Sometime we give ourselves our own peer pressure when we listen to others talk about how they enjoy sex with their boyfriend or girlfriend, they make their lives seem sooooo exciting that we secretly started trying to teach ourselves about anything and everything. <u>GALATIONS 5:19</u> PEOPLES DESIRES MAKE THEM GIVE INTO IMMORAL WAYS, FILTHY THOUGHTS AND SHAMEFUL DEEDS. Being a single parent to two sons, I should have been shocked when I found Pornographic magazines while cleaning, I never once thought about how long they had been looking at them or even how they got them. I was too busy celebrating my boy's aint soft yaaaa!! Never did it occur to me they could be sexually active at young ages, to me my thought was they would know what a woman's body looks like and wasn't any harm in them just looking at pictures, I'm a woman I can't teach them how to be a man. How wrong was that? Very wrong! I was allowing them to teach themselves when it came to their personal body parts and functions. I didn't know any better, I wasn't taught what the Bible said about sex. Me and my two sisters weren't allowed to have boys or anyone for that matter in my parent's house when they were gone except our brother or male cousins. When our parents were gone we didn't listen, we would sneak and have company over, boys and girls it didn't matter who it was, we knew it was wrong because we had a look out person who would start yelling THEY'RE HOME!!!! And everyone would clear the house including jumping over fences to keep from being caught by the parents we were all team players then looking out for each other, my parents, your parents anybody's parents, being caught we knew meant trouble on the B-hind and we wouldn't be able to go outside, back then not being able to go outside was a death sentence unlike children today hardly ever outside, also we would be punished with going to bed way before it got dark outside, those were real punishments, not take away your phone for a week or off the computer or Playstation. We can all think back to that feeling of fear we had of our parents and that greatest fear was getting a whoopin, not a spankin y'all know we got straight-up whoopins and Ya Bet Not Run!! (lol). Our parents weren't afraid to give out some Good Ole Act Right.

We were also taught what goes on in this house stays in this house, but when the parent's decided to stop raising their children everything was told going on in each other's houses. We parent's the ones who got our behinds adjusted on a regular basis were the first to say especially the young women, "When I grow up and have children I'm not gonna bring them up the way I was raised." We should have been saying, When I grow up and get married this is what I want to do and how I want my child to be raised. For the majority of us our parents were not being cruel, when we did something wrong they punished us according to what we did and how wrong it was, fighting with somebody, saying wrong things out ya mouth like cussing and repeating what ya heard while looking down grown-ups mouth, your parent would tell you don't get yo teeth knocked down your throat of don't get yo eyes knocked to the back of your head, lying and stealing. If you were a girl you couldn't talk on the phone with a boy until you reached a certain age and your first real date was to the school prom. Everything we did was usually a group thing, skating, bowling, going to the movies and the football or basketball games with our neighborhood, school and church friends.

Our parents noticed we weren't children anymore when the boys started getting bass in their voices, growing hair on their face and chest while the girls were getting shapes like their mother's worrying about the clothes they wear and not wanting pig tails or pony tails with their natural hair. The rules changed cause our parents were afraid somebody's gonna come up pregnant. When we asked to go somewhere the answer became no or let me think about it or I'll see, and when you got all that it usually meant no with why you can't because maybe it was your grades or you didn't do one of your house chores or you clowned at church which was talking or laughing while church was in service. The next thing came out our mouth was I'm bored we aint got nothing to do and your parent didn't care, but the sad thing about this, they did care by setting the morals they wanted us to live by in this worldly world which was simple to them they thought. To protect us from the world we should have been drilled over and over and over again until we really got it on how to live spiritual in a worldly world.

Read <u>COLOSSIANS 3:5,6</u> (5) DON'T BE CONTROLLED BY YOUR BODY KILL EVERY DESIRE FOR THE WRONG KIND OF SEX DON'T BE IMMORAL OR INDECENT(bad unclean corrupt) OR HAVE EVIL THOUGHTS DON'T BE GREEDY WHICH IS THE SAME AS WORSHIPPING IDOLS.(6) GOD IS ANGRY WITH PEOPLE WHO DISOBEY HIM BY DOING THESE THINGS.

Phone sex involves talking inappropriately (nasty) about sex or listening to inappropriate (nasty) messages on the phone. Sexting is when you use your cell phone to send naked pictures and text messages to other people. Cybersex is sexual interaction on the internet (having sex), these modern day electronics encourage people to experience sex way before getting married. Instead of controlling our urges for sex some people look for ways to satisfy their needs by going online, buying sex tools that look like parts of our bodies, they use lotions and potions, whips and chains. Then we have the strip dancers showing off the same naked skin to the same nasty man that's been coming for many generations before they got to the stage for them to be a mat so they can wipe their feet on after the feeling of being satisfied to their sexual needs. Masturbation which is deliberate self-stimulation (you do it yourself) that gives you sexual arousal and orgasm, a lot of men and women but for the most men have masturbated, it was said there is nothing wrong with it and that it was normal but again read <u>COLOSSIANS 3 ;5,6</u> where it shows us it is wrong.

<u>ROMANS 8:5,6</u> (5) PEOPLE ARE RULED BY THEIR DESIRES THINK ONLY OF THEMSELVES, EVERYONE WHO IS RULED BY THE HOLY SPIRIT THINK ABOUT SPIRITUAL THINGS, (6) IF OUR MINDS ARE RULED BY OUR DESIRES WE WILL DIE, BUT IF ARE MINDS ARE RULED BY THE SPIRIT WE WILL HAVE A LIFE OF PEACE

Our sexuality is not our own it is a gift of God to be treasured. Some of us think that the Bible has to many rules to live by or that you been living like this for so long aint nothing happened to me yet I'm still here. The reason why you are still here is. <u>ROMANS 1:24</u> GOD LET THESE PEOPLE GO THEIR OWN WAY THEY DID WHAT THEY WANTED TO DO, THEIR FILTHY THOUGHTS MADE THEM DO SHAMEFUL THINGS TO THEIR BODIES WITH ONE ANOTHER.

The world has accepted the Gay lifestyle, laws have been passed giving them rights to marry each other becoming male husband with male wife and female husband with female wife, both sets either have children from previous relationships of the female wife and female husband decide to have relations with a real man long enough to get pregnant then the real man gets kicked to the curb, his services are no longer needed, the child will never know his or her father for being raised by two mothers or two fathers who want the child to think its natural or ok. The laws allowed the adoption of children to people living this lifestyle they are trying to raise a family with only the values of the world. Who said it was a sin and that we could go to eternal fire as well as other offenders? GOD! I must say I've thought about this subject of what the Bible says about sex.

Why don't the preachers speak on this subject a little louder a lot clearer and with more emphasis? I'm blessed to have a Pastor and Evangelist that aren't shy about speaking on this subject, nor do they whisper maybe it's for fear of the membership leaving the church. I know a lot of people get mad at the Pastor or Teacher for preaching and showing us what we are doing or how we are living is a sin and that we could go to eternal fire (hell) instead of being thankful for the truth we wanna stop coming to church, Out of ear shot out of mind . . .

Fornication is Sexual Intercourse between partners who are not married. 1 THESSALOIANS 4:3

GOD WANTS YOU TO BE HOLY SO DON'T BE IMMORAL IN MATERS OF SEX. (stay away from sexual sin)

1 CORINTHIANS 6:18 KEEP FAR AWAY FROM SEXUAL SINS, ALL OTHER SINS A PERSON COMMITS ARE OUTSIDE HIS BODY, BUT SEXUAL SINS ARE SINS AGAINST ONES OWN BODY.

EPHESIANS 5:3 THERE SHOULD NOT BE EVEN A HINT OF SEXUAL SIN AMONG YOU, DON'T DO ANYTHING UNCLEAN, AND DO NOT ALWAYS WANT MORE AND MORE, THINGS LIKE THAT ARE NOT WHAT GOD'S HOLY PEOPLE SHOULD DO.

EPHESIANS 5:5 HERE IS WHAT YOU CAN BE SURE OF, THOSE WHO GIVE THEMSELVES OVER TO SEXUAL SINS ARE LOST, SO ARE PEOPLE WHOSE LIVES ARE NOT PURE. THE SAME IS TRUE OF THOSE WHO ALWAYS WANT MORE AND MORE, PEOPLE WHO DO THOSE THINGS MIGHT AS WELL WORSHIP STATUES OR gods, NO ONE WHO DOES THEM WILL RECEIVE A SHARE IN THE KINGDOM OF CHRIST AND GOD.

REVELATION 21:8 BUT OTHERS WILL HAVE THEIR PLACE IN THE LAKE OF FIRE THAT BURNS SULFER, THOSE WHO ARE AFRAID AND THOSE WHO DO NOT BELIEVE WILL BE THERE, MURDERERS AND THOSE WHO

PRACTICE WITCHCRAFT WILL GO THERE, THOSE WHO WORSHIP STATUES OF gods AND ALL WHO TELL LIES WILL BE THERE TO IT IS THE SECOND DEATH.

<u>1 THESSALONIANS 4:4,5</u> [4] HE WANTS ALL OF YOU TO LEARN TO CONTROL YOUR OWN BODIES, YOU MUST LIVE IN A WAY THAT IS HOLY, YOU MUST LIVE WITH HONOR. [5] DON'T LONG TO COMMIT SEXUAL SINS LIKE THOSE WHO DON'T KNOW GOD.

The Bible shows us that we should have control over our sexuality which means holding off on having sex which is worth the wait until the right time. Sometimes we make an excuse or justify why we are having sexual relations before marriage, here it goes again, we want to say everybody's doing it! No not everyone is doing it, some of us do hold on to our moral standards of living even without physical or mental struggles, we want to believe that even if we are not having sexual intercourse there is nothing wrong with being sexually intimate with someone if you are not married. The Bible says sexual uncleanness and loose conduct are different kinds of sexual intimacy and when we do these things when we are not married even when there is no intercourse (sex) this type of behavior is offensive to God. Sexual relations are only allowed to a man and a woman who are married to each other. The Bible disapproves of a covetous sexual appetite (for example) this applies to both man and woman. A woman doesn't have sex with her boyfriend but still does other forms of sex with him, by doing that they are coveting or lusting after something that does not belong to either of them which makes them guilty of sexual greed which is condemned in the Bible.

COLOSSIANS 3:5,6 (5) SO PUT TO DEATH ANYTHING THAT BELONGS TO YOUR EARTHLY NATURE, GET RID OF YOUR SEXUAL SINS AND UNCLEAN ACTS, DON'T LET YOUR FEELINGS GET OUT OF CONTROL, REMOVE FROM YOUR LIFE ALL EVIL LONGINGS,

STOP ALWAYS WANTING MORE AND MORE YOU MIGHT AS WELL BE WORSHIPPING STATUES OF gods. [6] GOD'S ANGER IS GOING TO COME BECAUSE OF THESE THINGS.

We have been in a world so wrapped up in our feelings and emotions we try to design how we want our lives to be with a certain man or woman. I had my life mapped out in my head how my house was gonna be, how my man (notice I didn't say my husband) was gonna have a nice physic with big muscles and a big paycheck, I did get what I wanted but I failed at the marriage part. I was one of many young women who had children without the thought of being married to their fathers even though it should have been just one father too. A lot of us young women gave up the most valuable prize we could give a man just because we thought it was love and that it was ok to be with him until ya'll called it quits then came another relationship to work at again only to become a single parent steady looking for love in all the wrong places. What I'm about to share was written in a book by two men, the wiser of the two wrote these words some of us should of read when we were little girls or wore them engraved inside a locket around our neck. It's hard to find love if your . . . (L) egs (O)pen (V)ery (E)asily . . . Don't get upset and say I wasn't a mannish girl! I wasn't either but instead of knowing what is love over being truly in love enough to wait for marriage was something I failed to do. Don't go looking for something that's not there, you will know when it's right cause it will come from Our Lord and Savior Jesus Christ at the right time. If it's a husband you want, if it's a wife you want ask and you shall receive. I hadn't asked for a husband because I didn't think it was wrong to have a boyfriend or man as long as he wasn't a married man, I thought it was alright to have babies with my man. When I got pregnant like a lot of us young women we would be the first to holler my miracle baby even though some weren't miracles even though they are a blessing, the relationship isn't being blessed by God until he blesses it. The Bible says stay as far as you can from anything that could lure you into sexual sin, I order you to remain morally clean, it is important for unmarried people to avoid getting close to getting into relationships with a man or woman who ignore God's views related to or concerning sex.

1 CORINTHIANS 7:9 BUT IF YOU CAN'T CONTROL YOURSELVES YOU SHOULD GET MARRIED, IT IS BETTER TO GET MARRIED THAN TO BURN WITH SEXUAL LONGING.

1 CORINTHIANS 7:2-5

(2) BUT SINCE THERE IS SO MUCH SEXUAL SIN, EACH MAN SHOULD HAVE HIS OWN WIFE, AND EACH WOMAN SHOULD HAVE HER OWN HUSBAND. (3) A HUSBAND SHOULD SATISFY HIS WIFES SEXUAL NEEDS AND A WIFE SHOULD SATISFY HER HUSBANDS NEEDS. (4) THE WIFES BODY DOES NOT BELONG ONLY TO HER, IT BELONGS TO HER HUSBAND IN THE SAME WAY THE HUSBANDS BODY DOES NOT BELONG ONLY TO HIM IT ALSO BELONGS TO HIS WIFE. (5) YOU SHOULDN'T STOP GIVING YOURSELVES TO EACH OTHER EXCEPT WHEN YOU BOTH AGREE TO DO SO AND THAT SHOULD BE ONLY TO GIVE YOURSELVES TIME TO PRAY

AWHILE, THEN YOU SHOULD COME TOGETHER AGAIN.

Sex and passion is a strong feeling and a beautiful thing but to keep from being active before your time you need a commitment toward being a husband and wife the Bible demands that commitment. You can enjoy the gift of sexual pleasure when a man and woman marry and come together emotionally and spiritually it is then they can get physical and be feely touchy and have all the tingly googly feelings they want.

MATTHEW   19:4-6   JESUS ANWERED, DON'T YOU KNOW THAT IN THE BEGINNING THE CREATOR MADE A MAN AND

A WOMAN? THAT'S WHY A MAN LEAVES HIS FATHER AND MOTHER AND GETS MARRIED, HE BECOMES LIKE ONE PERSON WITH HIS WIFE. THEN THEY ARE NO LONGER TWO PEOPLE BUT ONE. AND <u>NO ONE</u> SHOULD SEPARATE A COUPLE THAT GOD HAS JOINED TOGETHER.

<u>ECCLESIASTES 4:12</u> THOUGH ONE MAY BE OVER POWERED, TWO CAN DEFEND THEMSELVES. A CORD OF THREE STRANDS IS NOT QUICKLY BROKEN

A husband and wife that also have a commitment to God has the strength of a braid that when all three are braided together it's not easily broken, the husband is on the left the wife on the right and God in the middle, to get to the wife the husband must go pass God just as the wife must go past God to get to her husband.

<u>HEBREWS 13:4</u> MARRIAGE SHOULD BE HONORED BY ALL, AND THE BED KEPT PURE, FOR GOD WILL JUDGE THE ADULTERER ALL THE SEXUALLY IMMORAL (UNCLEAN) In other words respect your wedding vows be faithful to each other.

Adultery is breaking a marriage promise of vow by having sexual relations with someone other than your husband or wife.

EXODUS20:14/DEUTERONOMY 5:18 YOU SHALL NOT COMMIT ADULTERY

MATTHEW 5:27,28 (27) YOU KNOW THE COMMANDMENT WHICH SAYS BE FAITHFUL IN MARRIAGE. (28) BUT I TELL YOU THAT IF YOU LOOK AT ANOTHER WOMAN AND WANT HER YOU ARE ALREADY UNFAITHFUL IN YOUR THOUGHTS.

PROVERBS 5;15-19 (15) YOU SHOULD BE FAITHFUL TO YOUR WIFE JUST AS YOU TAKE WATER FROM A WELL (16) AND DON'T BE LIKE A STREAM FROM WHICH ANY WOMAN MAY TAKE A DRINK (17) SAVE YOURSELF FOR YOUR WIFE AND DON'T HAVE SEX WITH OTHER WOMEN. (18) BE HAPPY

WITH YOUR WIFE YOU MARRIED WHEN YOU WERE YOUNG. [19] SHE IS BEAUTIFUL AND GRACEFUL JUST LIKE A DEER YOU SHOULD BE ATTRACTED TO HER AND STAY DEEPLY IN LOVE.

I think if couples that want to be married should have a information packet of scriptures, I believe if they knew what God expects of them we would have a lot more happily married people like the couples in the church I attend, the real love they have and show for one another from the oldest couple to the youngest shows me and the other single men and women that true solid marriages still do exist. I tip my hat with gratitude to know them. Now where were we? Oh Adultery ok men read this with your wife next to you.

ECCLESIASTES 7:26 I DISCOVERED A BAD WOMAN IS WORSE THAN DEATH SHE IS A TRAP REACHING OUT WITH BODY AND SOUL TO CATCH YOU, BUT IF YOU OBEY GOD YOU CAN ESCAPE, IF YOU DON'T OBEY YOU ARE DONE FOR

PROVERBS 5:3-8 THE WORDS OF AN IMMORAL (adultress) WOMAN MAYBE AS SWEET AS HONEY AND AS SMOOTHE AS OLIVE OIL. BUT ALL YOU REALLY GET FROM BEING WITH HER IS BITTER POISON AND PAIN, IF YOU FOLLOW HER SHE WILL LEAD YOU DOWN TO THE

WORLD OF THE DEAD, SHE HAS MISSED THE PATH TO LIFE AND DOESN'T KNOW IT, STAY AWAY FROM A BAD WOMAN! DON'T EVEN GO NEAR THE DOOR OF HER HOUSE.

PROVERBS 6:26,29 (26) A WOMAN WHO SELLS HER LOVE CAN BE BOUGHT FOR AS LITTLE AS THE PRICE OF A MEAL. BUT MAKING LOVE TO ANOTHER MANS WIFE WILL COST YOU EVERYTHING. (29) AND IF YOU GO TO BED WITH ANOTHER MANS WIFE YOU PAY THE PRICE.

PROVERBS 6:32 BUT IF YOU GO TO BED WITH ANOTHER MAN'S WIFE YOU WILL DESTROY YOURSELF BY YOUR OWN STUPIDITY

I'm gonna tell you a story: From the window of my house I once happened to see some foolish men. It was late in the evening, sometime after dark. One of these young men turned the corner and was walking be the house of a unfaithful wife. She was dressed fancy like a woman of the street with only one thing in mind. She was one of those women who are loud and restless and never stay at home, who walked street after street waiting to trap a man. She grabbed him and kissed him and with no sense of shame she said, I had to offer a sacrifice and there is enough meat left over for a feast so I came looking for you, and here you are! The sheets on my bed are bright-colored cloth from

Egypt and I have covered it with perfume made of myrrh, aloes, and cinnamon. Let's go there and make love all night, my husband is traveling and he's far away, he took a lot of money along and he won't be back home before the middle of the month, And so, she tricked him with all her sweet talk and her flattery, Right away he followed her like an ox on the way to be slaughtered, or a fool on the way to be punished and killed with arrows. He was no more than a bird rushing into a trap without knowing it would cost him his life. My son pay close attention to what I have said. Don't even think about that kind of woman or let yourself be misled by someone like her, such a woman has caused the downfall and destruction of a lot of men. Her house is a one-way street leading straight down to the world of the dead. This story is in the Bible it can be found at <u>PROVERBS 7:6-27</u>

It's sad when a married couple has been together 10, 15, 20+ years and wake up one morning and don't want the commitment anymore, some say they got bored, they stayed together until the children got old enough. Others just wanted to do their own thing, start over looking for a way to be happy with themselves again, a lot of couples thought their marriage was just fine when all the while the husband was out chasing other women or the wife was sneaking around with another man, both having a spouse and family at home. No one stopped to imagine the pain of the married woman who's trying not to picture her husband in the arms of another woman as she stares at the clock ticking by with tears running down her face lying next to an empty pillow and the place where loved one should be or the husband pacing the floor wondering what was it he has done wrong hoping his wife doesn't stay out all night hanging on to another man's arm.

How should the children feel when they see their parents going through the issues they have? The man's son learns from his father to do a woman any kind of way he wants for watching how his mother was treated by his father and the daughter learns from the mother who doesn't stay at home to dress up look good paint your face and hit the street, look for the party where all the men are at, and we wonder how our young men walk around disrespecting women with their pants hanging off their B-hinds with belts huggin the knees walking all crazy kinds a ways just to keep them from falling to the ground and the young women selling their bodies on street corners and strip clubs.

This generation we live in now the women never think about how wrong it is to sleep with or even have a baby by a married man that already has a family. The boyfriend and girlfriend of today are having sexual relations trying to have a baby purposely and living together calling each other family with no thoughts of getting married. I encourage you to go back and read the scriptures written in these pages on what the Bible says about sex, study them believe what is said and what can happen to you if you choose to continue living this way.

Covet is to want of have a desire for someone or something another person has.

EXODUS 20:17 DO NOT WANT ANYTHING THAT BELONGS TO SOMEONE ELSE DON'T WANT

ANYONE'S HOUSE, WIFE, OR HUSBAND, SLAVES, OXEN, DONKEYS OF ANYTHING ELSE.

Everything I mean everything we all have doesn't really belong to us, our cars, houses, jobs and even our very own bodies don't belong to us. When we go out and purchase things with our money we say it's mine. When we look through the window at the birth of our child, we say it's mine but in all actuality we don't even own a thing, It <u>All</u> belongs to God, he blesses us with all these things. Some of us are just never satisfied with what we have, we want to keep up with the Hadley family.

MARK 7:20-23 THEN JESUS SAID WHAT COMES FROM YOUR HEART IS WHAT MAKES YOU UNCLEAN, OUT OF YOUR HEART COME EVIL THOUGHTS, VULGAR DEEDS, STEALING, MURDER, UNFAITHFULNESS IN MARRIAGE, GREED, MEANNESS, DECEIT, INDECENCY, ENVY, INSULTS, PRIDE AND FOOLISHNESS, ALL OF THESE COME FROM YOUR HEART AND THEY ARE WHAT MAKE YOU UNFIT TO WORSHIP GOD.

Many people in our world today think we should be able to live without having to suffer from anything that caused pain and disappointments. We do anything we want, we think our pleasures and happiness is our right that we have. We feel nothing can stop us from getting our own personal desires and that life owes us that much. We have so much going on in our lives we don't have time to think or hear about the things we can't or won't except or control. We make up excuses to keep from thinking or asking ourselves the question what I'm doing is a sin, its wrong and I could burn in hell forever. We don't like to admit we have problems instead we tell each other I'm alright everything is fine. We want everyone to believe that life is great even when we are going through something.

When we know about the pain and problems someone is going

through, some of us just don't care, only thing they can manage to say is "Life's Hard" instead of telling them about the happiness God gives. A lot of people in the world now have nothing on their mind but living from one day to the next, one party after another, they don't blame themselves for their actions they did the night before, they blame it on the alcohol, which is the cause of a lot of coveting but it's not the alcohols fault, it's the person who chose to participate, trying to be the life of the party. The Bible also warns us about the dangers of alcohol read <u>PROVERBS 23:35</u> WHO IS ALWAYS IN TROUBLE? WHO ARGUES AND FIGHTS? WHO HAS CUTS AND BRUISES? WHOSE

EYES ARE RED? EVERYONE WHO STAYS UP LATE HAVING JUST ONE MORE DRINK, DON'T EVEN LOOK AT THAT COLORFUL STUFF BUBBLING UP IN THE GLASS! IT GOES DOWN EASILY, BUT LATER IT BITES LIKE A POSIONOUS SNAKE. YOU WILL SEE WEIRD THINGS AND YOU MIND WILL PLAY TRICKS ON YOU, YOU WILL FEEL TOSSED ABOUT LIKE SOMEONE TRYING TO SLEEP ON A SHIP IN A STORM.

We shouldn't compare our sins to other people's sins we can't make our sins right in our thoughts either. We should accept our own weaknesses of our sins, repent (apologize of be sorry for what you have done) and turn away of stop doing the things that cause you to sin. Jesus will forgive you if you ask him to with a humble truthful heart because he died for you and me to save us from all our sins.

2 CORINTHIANS 5:17,18 ANYONE WHO BELONGS TO CHRIST (Jesus) IS A NEW PERSON. THE PAST IS FORGOTTEN AND EVERYTHING IS NEW. GOD HAS DONE IT ALL! HE SENT CHRIST TO MAKE PEACE BETWEEN HIMSELF AND US, AND HE HAS GIVEN US THE WORK OF MAKING PEACE BETWEEN HIMSELF AND OTHERS

God created us with a mind to be able to think and remember things that have happened in our lives. When you think back to the events of your life a year ago to now, if you are at the same place in your life such as you don't have a job, you don't have a roof over your head, you haven't stopped using drugs or excessive drinking or you haven't forgiven someone for the wrongs they did to you, maybe it's time for you to change by asking God Our Heavenly Father to help you with these changes and coming to him with the belief that with God all things are possible.

GALATIONS 5:16,17 IF YOU ARE GUIDED BY THE SPIRIT YOU WONT OBEY YOUR SELFISH DESIRES. THE SPIRIT AND YOU DESIRES ARE ENEMIES OF EACH OTHER.

THEY ARE ALWAYS FIGHTING EACH OTHER AND KEEPING YOU FROM DOING WHAT YOU FEEL YOU SHOULD

GALATIONS 5:24-26 AND BECAUSE WE BELONG TO CHRIST JESUS, WE HAVE KILLED OUR SELFISH FEELINGS AND DESIRES. GODS SPIRIT HAS GIVEN US LIFE AND SO WE SHOULD FOLLOW THE SPIRIT, BUT DON'T BE CONCEITED OR MAKE OTHERS JEALOUS BY CLAIMING TO BE BETTER THAN THEY ARE

If you have faith in Jesus you are a new person, the old things or habits, the places you go and some of the people you hung out with and even your character (how you carry yourself) are done away with you know longer do. You have become entirely a different person, an improved new you who shows love by being kind, patient, never jealous or boastful, never rude of selfish, doesn't have a temper, don't keep up with who did you wrong. Having a new character you should be loving, happy, faithful, honest and have self-control, trusting and supportive to anyone that needs it.

ROMANS 3:23 ALL OF US HAVE SINNED AND FALLEN SHORT OF GODS GLORY (Gods Glory)

We all have heard the time is drawing near and we know what that means. God will judge us on what we have done with the dash in the middle of our lives, which is the beginning (your birth) to the end (your death) whether it's good or bad. This world as we know it will soon be over, look all around us the signs are already here, we are living in the last days some people are saying how do you know? Let's see what the Bible says read <u>2 TIMOTHY 3:1-5</u> YOU CAN BE CERTAIN THAT IN THE LAST DAYS THERE WILL BE SOME VERY HARD TIMES. PEOPLE WILL LOVE ONLY THEMSELVES AND MONEY. THEY WILL BE PROUD, STUCK-UP, RUDE, AND DISOBEDIANT TO THEIR PARENTS. THEY WILL ALSO BE UNGRATEFUL, GODLESS, HEARTLESS AND HATEFUL THEIR WORDS WILL BE CRUEL,

AND THEY WILL HAVE NO SELF-CONTROL OR PITY. THESE PEOPLE WILL HATE EVERYTHING THAT IS GOOD. THEY WILL BE SNEAKY, RECKLESS AND PUFFED UP WITH PRIDE. INSTEAD OF LOVING GOD, THEY WILL LOVE PLEASURE EVEN THOUGH THEY WILL MAKE A SHOW OF BEING RELIGIOUS, THEIR RELIGION WON'T BE REAL. DON'T HAVE ANYTHING TO DO WITH SUCH PEOPLE.

Back to the reason for the pages written on the subject about what the Bible says about sex a reminder on what you should pay attention to in regards to your children. Mothers and Fathers when your daughter of son has an interest in a boy or girl this is the time that sex would enter their minds, Let them know they are not ready, explain why, show them what the Bible says, help them focus on making good decisions, Let them know that they can talk to you or ask questions about anything including sex. Have information available to them that they can depend on you for. Don't be afraid to talk about the risks they are taking show your support.

COLOSSIANS 3:21 PARENTS DON'T BE HARD ON YOUR CHILDREN, IF YOU ARE THEY MIGHT GIVE UP.

It's not easy to talk to our children on some subjects especially when it comes to sex. Some of the reasons are a lot of us weren't taught. Back when I was growing up nobody talked about sex or any type of changes our bodies would go through. The women's ministry at the church I attend. We shared what we went through when we started our cycles. One story one of the sisters shared was she thought she was pregnant, I shared when it happened to me I thought I was dying, we shared a few laughs about our bodies going through these changes and how troublesome it really was to have nobody telling us anything or what to expect. Some of our parents were just too embarrassed sex was a subject that made them feel uncomfortable. If only I was taught, I would of made better choices, I thought having sex made a relationship stronger, but when the relationship was over I knew I wasn't in love, just wanted to make love. Now I can truly say I know better, reading the Bible and studying has shown me the truth about sex and many other things on how we should live.

If you let God take control of your life you won't have a lot of troubles, I didn't say we won't go through something but when we do remember God is there, remember he won't leave us or forsake us. When you feel things are going against you or when a little something happens to you don't give up, don't be so quick to throw in the towel whenever something goes wrong remember to pray, when you done all you can and there's nothing left to do Pray!

While you are still here in this world you need to make up your mind whose child you belong to Our Heavenly Father of the child of Satan (The Devil) I like the words my Pastor said in a sermon he preached. If you choose Satan (The Devil) to be your Father, you are choosing Hell to be your Home!

EPHESIANS 4:22-24 YOU WERE TOLD THAT YOUR FOOLISH DESIRES WILL DESTROY YOU, AND THAT YOU MUST GIVE UP

YOUR OLD WAY OF LIFE WITH ALL ITS BAD HABITS LET THE SPIRIT CHANGE YOUR WAY OF THINKING AND MAKE YOU A NEW PERSON YOU WERE CREATED TO BE LIKE GOD AND SO YOU MUST PLEASE HIM AND BE TRULY HOLY

<u>1 TIMOTHY 6:7,8</u> WE DIDN'T BRING ANYTHING INTO THIS WORLD, AND WE WON'T TAKE ANYTHING WITH US WHEN WE LEAVE SO WE SHOULD BE SATISFIED JUST TO HAVE FOOD AND CLOTHES

Here are some more words spoken from a message my Pastor preached, It's time to reshape your life for the word of God.

I end these pages with the hope that these words have touched someone even if it's just one person this work would not be in vain. My prayer is that this tool will be used to touch many that don't even realize the way they are living will not get your seat into the Kingdom God has prepared for us. May you read these pages with an open mind and heart to receive its message it brings Amen.

www.ingramcontent.com/pod-product-compliance
Lightning Source LLC
Chambersburg PA
CBHW050412290526
45786CB00003B/1236